Where Is
the Grand Canyon?

by Jim O'Connor

illustrated by Daniel Colón

Grosset & Dunlap
An Imprint of Penguin Group (USA) LLC

For Teddy, who asked me to visit the
Grand Canyon with him—JOC

For my parents, who taught
me to love the outdoors—DC

GROSSET & DUNLAP
Published by the Penguin Group
Penguin Group (USA) LLC, 375 Hudson Street, New York, New York 10014, USA

USA | Canada | UK | Ireland | Australia | New Zealand | India | South Africa | China

penguin.com
A Penguin Random House Company

Text copyright © 2015 by Jim O'Connor. Illustrations copyright © 2015 by Penguin Group (USA) LLC. All rights reserved. Published by Grosset & Dunlap, a division of Penguin Young Readers Group, 345 Hudson Street, New York, New York 10014. GROSSET & DUNLAP is a trademark of Penguin Group (USA) LLC. Printed in the USA.

Library of Congress Cataloging-in-Publication Data is available.

ISBN 978-0-448-48357-3   10 9 8 7 6 5 4 3 2 1

Contents

Where Is the Grand Canyon?

The Grand Canyon in Arizona is one of the United States' fifty-nine national parks. All are special wilderness areas that are protected by the US government. President Franklin Roosevelt said, "There is nothing so American as our national parks." Why? Because the parks belong to all the people of our country. They are not private property.

Back when the United States was a young country with limitless open space, not many people saw a need to set aside land for parks.

Even if there had been big parks, few people could have visited them. The majority of Americans worked six days a week. Not many had the time or money to travel more than a few miles from their home.

The first public park in the United States was the Boston Common, in Massachusetts, which was established in 1634. It was both a park and a common grazing area for cows.

In the 1830s, Americans began building cemeteries that were more than places to bury the dead. They had winding roads, ponds, landscaped hills, beautiful statues, and fancy mausoleums. (Mausoleums are like little houses with the dead buried inside them.)

People went to these beautiful cemeteries to have picnics and stroll around the grounds admiring the views. Cemeteries became popular as a kind of public park.

The idea of parks protected by the government began in the mid 1800s. The population was growing. More cities were sprouting all over the country, taking over large areas of land. A small

but important group of people realized that the United States had great natural treasures that needed to be preserved for all Americans forever.

For instance, Yosemite, an area in northern California, was known for its special trees. They were called giant sequoias. Some were over three thousand years old. They grew up to three hundred feet high with amazingly thick trunks. A group of Americans wanted to protect Yosemite's giant sequoia groves from logging and development. In 1864, President Abraham Lincoln made Yosemite a California state park.

The first area to be named a national park was Yellowstone in Wyoming. (Parts of the park are also in Montana and Idaho.)

Yellowstone is a special place because it is home to most of the world's geysers. A geyser is an underground spring of boiling-hot water that erupts through the surface of the earth. Yellowstone's most famous geyser is called Old

Faithful. In fact, it is the most famous geyser in the world. Every ninety-one minutes, Old Faithful erupts, spraying water 125 feet into the air. Yellowstone National Park was created in 1872 under a law signed by President Ulysses S. Grant.

The US Army

In the early days, Yellowstone and other national parks like Yosemite and Glacier in Montana were supervised by the United States Army. But army troops only spent the summer months in the parks. During the rest of the year, troops carried out their duties as soldiers. With only part-time help, it was very difficult to plan and complete long-term projects in the parks. So, in 1916, Congress created the National Park Service to supervise all the national parks.

The president who did the most for national parks was Theodore Roosevelt. He was in office from 1901 to 1909 and is often called the "conservation president." He wanted to conserve—keep and protect—the beauty of nature in the United States.

President Roosevelt grew up in New York City, but he was a real outdoorsman. As a young man, he became a cattle rancher out west in North Dakota. All his life he loved to hunt and camp out under the stars. He wanted Americans and visitors from other countries to enjoy the beauty of the United States in its most unspoiled form.

More than a century ago Roosevelt saw how dangerous industry could be to natural resources such as water and forests. He said, "We have become great because of the lavish use of our resources. But the time has come to inquire seriously what will happen when our forests are gone, when the coal, the iron, the oil, and the gas are exhausted, when the soils have still further impoverished and washed into the streams, polluting the rivers, denuding the fields and obstructing navigation."

In 1903 he visited the Grand Canyon.

Here's his description: "In the Grand Canyon, Arizona has a natural wonder which is in kind absolutely unparalleled throughout the rest of the world." By that, he meant there was no place else like it. Roosevelt said, "You cannot improve on it.

The ages have been at work on it, and man can only mar it."

In the summer of 1913, Roosevelt returned to the Grand Canyon with his sons Archie and Quentin. During their vacation, they rode horses along the rim of the canyon and hunted cougars. Roosevelt wrote about his trip, calling the Grand Canyon "the most wonderful scenery in the world." He said, "Very wealthy men can have private game preserves of their own. But the average man . . . can enjoy wild nature, only if . . .

there are big parks or reserves provided for the use of all our people."

In 1919, Grand Canyon became a national park.

National Parks

Wrangell-St. Elias in Alaska is our largest national park. It covers over thirteen million acres. (That is bigger than the states of Maryland and Delaware combined.) American Samoa National Park is the smallest, with only 13,500 acres. Four thousand five hundred acres of that park are underwater coral reefs. In terms of size, Grand Canyon is the eleventh-largest national park. However, it is the second-most visited, with five million tourists coming

Glacier

Yellowstone

Yosemite

Grand Canyon

Wrangell-St. Elias

every year. Great Smoky Mountains National Park in Tennessee and North Carolina is the most popular, with nine million visitors a year.

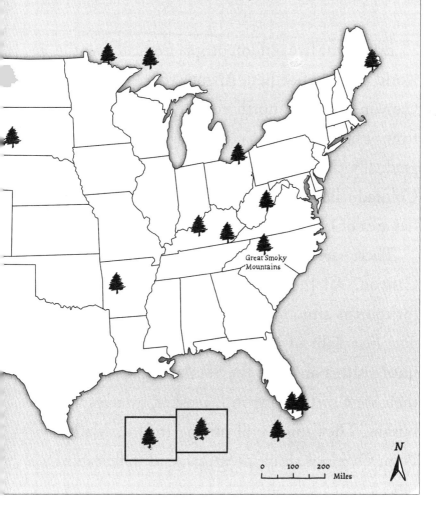

Great Smoky
Mountains

N

0   100   200
⊢——⊢——⊢——⊢   Miles

CHAPTER 1
Birth of a Canyon

Every year five million people from all over the world travel to northern Arizona to see the Grand Canyon. Driving north to the Grand Canyon from Phoenix, Sedona, or Flagstaff, the road gradually climbs to the top of what is called the Colorado Plateau. (A plateau is a large elevated flat area of land.)

There are plenty of signs for the Grand Canyon. All the hotels, restaurants, and stores for tourists announce that you are getting closer. The first sight of the canyon itself doesn't come until visitors arrive at the South Rim. Even then their view of the canyon is masked by trees and bushes. They must pull off the road at Mather Point Overlook, leave their cars, and walk a short

distance to the rim of the Grand Canyon. Then—
WOW! Suddenly they look down. People cannot
help but gasp in surprise at what they see.

What Is a Canyon?

A canyon is a deep, steep-sided gorge that is usually created by erosion. Sometimes earthquakes contribute to the formation of canyons. The deepest canyon in the world is Yarlung Tsangpo Grand Canyon in Tibet. At one point, it is sixteen thousand feet deep. That is more than three miles. The longest canyon in the world was discovered in 2013. It is hidden beneath a glacier in Greenland and goes for at least 460 miles. It has not even been named yet.

The Grand Canyon twists and turns for 270 miles. It is eighteen miles across at its widest point. This massive canyon was formed by the constant erosion of the Colorado River for the last six million years.

The river has cut through thousands of different layers of rock, so that now the canyon is over a mile deep. The "youngest" rock, near the top, is 250 million years old. The oldest—at the bottom—was formed two billion years ago.

As visitors gaze into the depths of the Grand Canyon, the shifting rays of the sun light up rock formations, smaller side canyons, and amazing colored layers of rock. Some are bright orange, some are golden brown, some are pink and white. Late in the day when the sun begins to set, the landscape turns violet, then darkens to purple before it disappears into the darkness.

At first glance, the Grand Canyon seems empty, but it is teeming with wildlife and countless varieties of plants. The scale is so huge that a boulder larger than a three-story building looks like a small rock to visitors at the rim. Even the mighty Colorado River seems tiny when seen from a mile above.

Seven Natural Wonders of the World

The Grand Canyon is listed as one of the Seven Natural Wonders of the World. There are many lists of World Wonders. They usually include the Great Wall of China, the Great Pyramids in Egypt, and whichever building is the tallest skyscraper at the time the list is made. All have one thing in common—they are man-made.

The seven greatest natural wonders have been created over millions of years as the earth formed and changed. Besides the Grand Canyon, here are the six others most people agree on:

The Great Barrier Reef in Australia is the largest coral reef in the world. Covering approximately 133,000 square miles, it is so large it can be seen from outer space.

Mount Everest is the highest mountain on earth.

Its summit is 29,029 feet high. Everest straddles the border of Tibet and Nepal.

Victoria Falls in Africa is the largest waterfall in the world. It is on the border of Zambia and Zimbabwe.

The auroras are natural light shows that occur high in the northern and southern skies. They usually look like green or purple curtains that pulse and change shape continuously.

Brazil's Great Harbor of Rio de Janeiro is the largest harbor in the world. It covers about four hundred square miles.

Paricutín in Mexico is a cinder cone volcano that suddenly began erupting in 1943 and continued until 1952. It is 1,391 feet tall and covers an area of about twenty square miles.

CHAPTER 2
Native People

Native Americans have lived in and around the canyon for at least the last ten thousand years.

The first humans to see the Grand Canyon were bands of hunters who roamed the American Southwest. When they first stood at the rim of the canyon, they would have looked at the same incredibly colorful rock formations seen today.

In fact, except for a few recent buildings scattered along the South Rim of the Grand Canyon, almost everything these ancient people saw looks the same now. Ten thousand years is just a blink of the eye in the formation of a canyon that is at least six million years old.

These first visitors were nomads who traveled and hunted throughout the Southwest. They did not build permanent homes or villages. Some of the animals they hunted still live in the Grand Canyon—deer, antelope, bighorn sheep, and rabbits.

The only trace these ancient people left behind are the spearheads they used for hunting bighorn sheep and deer. Archeologists call these people Paleo-Indians. Paleo means "ancient."

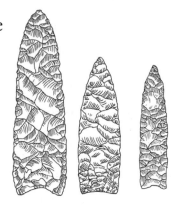

Between two thousand and four thousand years ago, other groups of nomadic hunters came to the canyon. They are called the Desert Culture, and they made figures of animals from willow twigs they split and bent. These figures were left in hundreds of limestone caves that are cut into the canyon's walls. They were probably gifts to their gods.

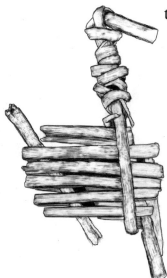
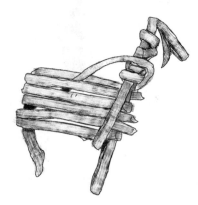

Some of these original split-twig figures are on display at the park's Tusayan Museum. Tusayan is the ruin of an eight-hundred-year-old village that was built by the Pueblo Indians. It is located about twenty-five miles east of Grand Canyon Village, near the Desert View Watchtower.

The next native people to live in the canyon were the Anasazi. They arrived on the Colorado Plateau roughly 1,500 years ago. Their name comes from the Navajo word that means "Ancient Ones" or "Ancient Enemy." The Anasazi were hunters and farmers. They hunted deer, antelope, and sheep. In the summer they planted corn, beans, and squash. They also gathered and ate piñon nuts, pods from yucca trees, and cactus fruit.

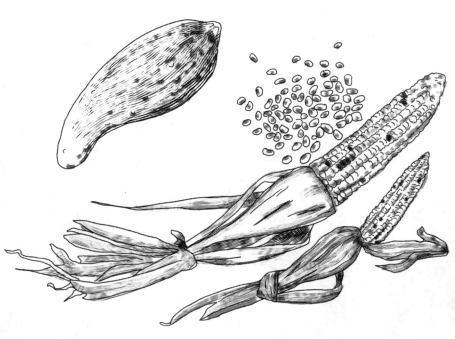

The Anasazi wove beautiful baskets and made sandals, clay bowls, and other items. In the winter they used deerskin and rabbit fur to make capes and blankets.

In the late twelfth century, a dry spell forced the Anasazi to abandon the Grand Canyon and move south and east to the Hopi Mesas and Rio Grande Valley.

Not long after the Anasazi left the Grand Canyon, other Native American tribes began to arrive. First came the Hopi. They have lived around the Grand Canyon for over a thousand years. One of their villages, Oraibi, is probably the oldest community in the United States—it's over eight hundred years old! Today Hopi Indians live on a small reservation surrounded by a much larger reservation belonging to Navajo Indians.

Navajo and Hopi Indians have lived near each other for centuries. There have been many disagreements between the two tribes. The Navajo became sheepherders starting in the late 1400s. That's when Spanish explorers first brought sheep to the Southwest. The Hopi, however, have always been farmers, raising crops such as corn and beans. They have resented sheep grazing because it ruins the land for farming.

Another tribe of hunters—the Southern Paiute—lived on the Kaibab plateau north of the canyon. (Kaibab means "mountain turned upside down" in the Paiute language.) They first came to the Grand Canyon around 1300 AD.

The Havasupai tribe's reservation land cuts right through the canyon. In fact, the Havasupai are the only tribe remaining in the canyon today. Their 188,077-acre reservation borders the western edge of Grand Canyon National Park. Their name means "people of the blue-green water." It refers to the blue Havasu Creek and its spectacular waterfalls. This is a popular but remote area. It can only be reached by hiking, by mule, or by helicopter. The Havasupai own and operate a hotel and campground near the creek and waterfalls.

The Zuni, who live in northern New Mexico today, also lived in the Grand Canyon. They have a unique language that is unlike any other Native American dialect.

Another canyon-area tribe is the Hualapai. Hualapai means "people of the tall pines." They have never lived in the canyon but hunt and farm west of the park. In 2007, they built Grand

Canyon Skywalk. It is a glass-bottom observation platform. It allows visitors to look straight down to the canyon floor. Tourists are amazed by the thrilling view.

However, for the Native Americans who have lived in the region for so long, the canyon is important for much more than its scenery. The Grand Canyon is a place filled with great spiritual meaning. The Zuni, for example, regard certain waterfalls in the canyon as sacred places.

Most Native American tribes believe in the Flood Myth—a story that tells of a new beginning for the world after a great flood. The Hopi believe that the flood took place at the Grand Canyon. Hopi men still make pilgrimages to the Grand Canyon. They come to collect salt from a mine near the Colorado River. The salt is used in their tribal rituals.

For all these native people, the Grand Canyon is first and foremost a sacred site, one that must be treated with respect and protected for future generations.

CHAPTER 3
Cities of Gold

In 1540, a group from Spain led by Francisco Vásquez de Coronado was exploring the southwest of North America. They were searching for the Seven Cities of Cíbola, which according to legend were filled with treasures.

Twenty years earlier, another explorer, Hernando Cortés, had conquered the Aztec people of Mexico. Cortés had sent incredible treasures home to Spain. Coronado believed that the seven cities with all their riches lay farther north in what is now Arizona. He wanted to send treasure back to Spain and be famous like Cortés.

Coronado's group found nothing more than a

small Native American village where the cities of gold were supposed to be. There was no treasure. Coronado, however, was not ready to give up. He sent out a search party to look farther west for the cities of Cíbola. These men had no success, either. But they did tell Coronado that there was a large and powerful river that might lead to the seven cities.

So Coronado sent out yet another search party. It was led by García López de Cárdenas. This group didn't find the cities of Cíbola, either.

What they did "discover," however, was the Grand Canyon. They were the first Europeans to lay eyes on it. When they looked down from the canyon's South Rim, the Spaniards thought that the river flowing far below was only six feet wide! How could this be the mighty river that they'd been sent to find? (In reality the Colorado averages three hundred feet across.)

Still, Cárdenas ordered some of the men to walk down into the canyon and look around. It was tough going. There was no trail down the steep canyon walls. As they got deeper into the canyon, the men realized the rocks that looked so small from up on the rim were, in fact, giant boulders. Some were almost two hundred feet high. (That's as tall as a twenty-story building.)

Finally the men gave up trying to reach the bottom of the canyon and climbed back up. They told Cárdenas what they had seen, and he decided to return to Coronado. That was the end of the search for the cities of gold. However, the Spanish continued to rule an area that is now Arizona, New Mexico, Texas, and southern California for another three hundred years.

The arrival of Spanish explorers had a major impact on native peoples in the area of the Grand Canyon. The Spanish brought horses, sheep, and cattle to the Southwest. This forever changed how native tribes lived and where they traveled.

It wasn't until 1776 that a Spanish priest named the canyon's river Colorado, which is Spanish for "colored red." When he saw the river for the first time, it was during the spring floods. Red silt had washed down from the desert, making the water look red.

The United States acquired the land that includes the Grand Canyon in 1803. It was part of what is called the Louisiana Purchase. President Thomas Jefferson bought a huge area of land for less than three cents an acre. Settlers, however, were more interested in the northern regions of the Louisiana Purchase. Animals like beaver and

Thomas
Jefferson

buffalo lived there.
They were valuable
for their fur.

Not until 1857
did the United States
government send a group
to explore the lower Colorado River. It was led
by Lieutenant Joseph Christmas Ives. Ives ran his
steamship, *Explorer,* aground many times until he
finally wrecked it. He was not at all impressed
by what he saw of the Grand Canyon. In a
report sent to Washington, DC, Ives wrote, "The
region . . . is, of course, altogether valueless."

Joseph Ives

CHAPTER 4
A One-Armed Adventurer

The first group to explore the Grand Canyon from end to end was led by John Wesley Powell in 1869. Powell had been a soldier in the Civil War. He had lost his right arm in battle. Powell's men always referred to him as "the Major."

John Wesley Powell

Powell was a geologist—he was interested in the study of rocks and the earth's layers. He was convinced that the Grand Canyon offered a great opportunity to study millions of years of the earth's history. He kept a detailed journal of everything he saw.

He took a group of nine men exploring in four wooden boats. They started on May 26, 1869, on Utah's Green River. They had enough supplies for ten months. Within the first month one boat was wrecked and half of the supplies were lost, so they were always short on food. One of the men quit and went home. Powell and the others continued in the remaining three boats.

Early in the trip Powell narrowly avoided a fatal fall. On July 8, Powell and another man named George Bradley decided to measure the height of the cliffs above the river. Even with just one arm, Powell had climbed cliffs many times. So had Bradley. They took no ropes or safety gear with them.

Powell and Bradley made steady progress until they were about six hundred feet above the river. Suddenly they began to have more difficulty finding a route to the top. Powell was leading. He edged out onto a narrow ledge and saw a place to hold above his head. With his one arm, Powell stretched and grabbed the rock. However, he quickly realized that he was trapped. If he let go of the rock, there was nothing else for him to hold on to.

There was no way to go, up or down.

Powell's muscles began to cramp. Bradley had no time to go for help. He had to act quickly to save Powell.

Luckily Bradley found a way to reach a ledge above Powell. He leaned over. Right away he realized that Powell was too far below him. He couldn't reach down to catch Powell's wrist.

Bradley had a sudden, desperate plan. He had climbed the cliff just wearing a shirt, pants, and long underwear. He stripped off his clothes and dangled the long underwear down to Powell. Powell had to let go of the rock and grab onto the underwear. He had to do it in an instant, and he would only have one chance. If he missed, he would fall to his death.

Luck was on Powell's side. He grabbed hold of the underwear and hung on until George Bradley pulled him up to the ledge he was on.

Later, back at camp, Bradley wrote in his diary, "Climbed the mountain this morning. Found it very hard one to ascend but we succeeded at last. In one place Major having but one arm couldn't get up so I took off my drawers and they made an excellent substitute for rope and with that assistance he got up safe."

Powell and his men did not reach the Colorado River until July 17. One day Powell and his men discovered a small stream flowing into the Colorado. Powell named it Bright Angel Creek because the water was clear and bright compared to the muddy brown Colorado. Today the main route from Grand Canyon Village down to the river is called Bright Angel Trail, as it ends right at this spot.

Powell and his men were traveling through uncharted waters. They had no idea where they were going or what lay ahead. It was very dangerous. There were hundreds of wild rapids that could easily turn their boats into toothpicks and drown all the men. No one in Powell's group had any experience running rapids.

Their boats were all wrong for the trip. They should have had light, flat-bottomed boats that would ride high in the water and glide over hidden rocks. Their boats, however, were heavy rowboats, called dories. Dories sat deep in the water and were hard to steer. Worst of all, the men rowed facing upstream. That meant they could not see where to steer when they hit rapids.

Whenever possible they portaged around dangerous rapids. "Portaging" means they carried the boats along the side of the canyon.

After three months, they came to the most dangerous-looking set of rapids yet. The canyon walls were sheer stone rising hundreds of feet. There was no way to portage.

Right then and there, three men decided to leave the expedition. Powell tried to persuade them to stay, but they would not change their minds. So Powell said good-bye and wished them well. The men set off to hike out of the canyon and were never seen again.

As luck would have it, Powell and the rest of his men had no difficulty getting through the rapids that day. (Powell named the spot Separation Rapids in honor of the men who left him there.) The following day, August 29, 1869, the Powell Expedition reached the very western end of the Grand Canyon.

Their journey was complete.

Death in the Grand Canyon

Like any wilderness area, the Grand Canyon can be dangerous if a person is not careful. The rough count is now around seven hundred deaths since tourists started coming to the Grand Canyon in the 1870s. Many times people get hurt because they do not use common sense. They stand too close to the edge of the canyon and fall. Or they don't take enough water on hikes. Animal attacks are very rare, and no one has ever died from a rattlesnake bite there.

The worst disaster at the park took place in 1956. Two airplanes collided over the canyon, killing all 128 passengers and crew.

The 1869 trip was not the only one Powell made to the area. He returned to the canyon several times. In 1871, he brought a photographer with him, who took some of the very first pictures of the Grand Canyon.

Powell kept a detailed journal of each trip and published the report. The book was called *Exploration of the Colorado River of the West and Its Tributaries*. (A tributary is a smaller river that flows into a bigger one.)

Powell became famous and gave many lectures about his adventures. His book brought lots of attention to the Grand Canyon. Before long, other Americans began exploring the canyon.

Miners came searching for copper, gold, or lead. Prospecting in the Grand Canyon was very difficult. Some of the miners gave up the hunt for metal and found a different way to make money. They started renting tents to tourists from back east. Before long the tent village was replaced by hotels.

In 1901, the Santa Fe Railroad ran a spur line to Grand Canyon Village. Now tourists could travel to the Grand Canyon easily instead of taking a bumpy eleven-hour stagecoach ride from Flagstaff, Arizona. The railroad company also built a fancy hotel. It was called the El Tovar and is still in business. By 1919, more than forty thousand tourists had visited the Grand Canyon in one year.

CHAPTER 5
A Layer Cake of Rock

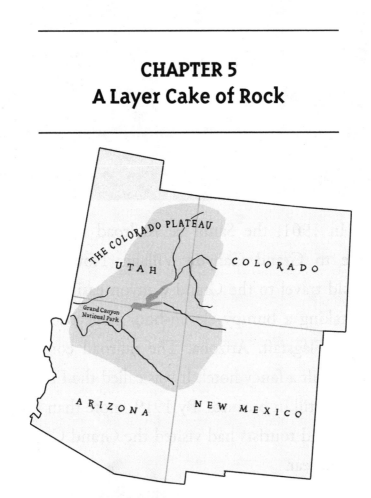

The Grand Canyon is located in a 130,000-square-mile region called the Colorado Plateau. The plateau covers northern Arizona, southern Utah, the southwest corner of Colorado, and part of northwest New Mexico. (It also contains ten national parks, including Grand Canyon.)

Most of the plateau consists of thousands of layers of sedimentary rock formed when ancient oceans covered the area. When the oceans disappeared, the plateau remained.

So how was the Grand Canyon made? The simple answer is erosion from the river. For millions of years the Colorado River cut its way through many layers of different rock. Little by little, the river sliced into the land—a slice that is nearly three hundred miles long and over a mile deep.

Erosion from the Colorado River, however, is not the only reason the canyon exists. The desert terrain of the Southwest does not encourage plant growth. Without plants and their root systems to hold soil, more erosion occurs.

Although the Southwest has an arid—or dry— climate, it does rain and snow at the canyon at times. And when it does, the storms are violent. Rainfall is hard, and this speeds erosion, too. The yearly winter rains run down the canyon walls and wash sand, pebbles, rocks, and boulders into the gorge.

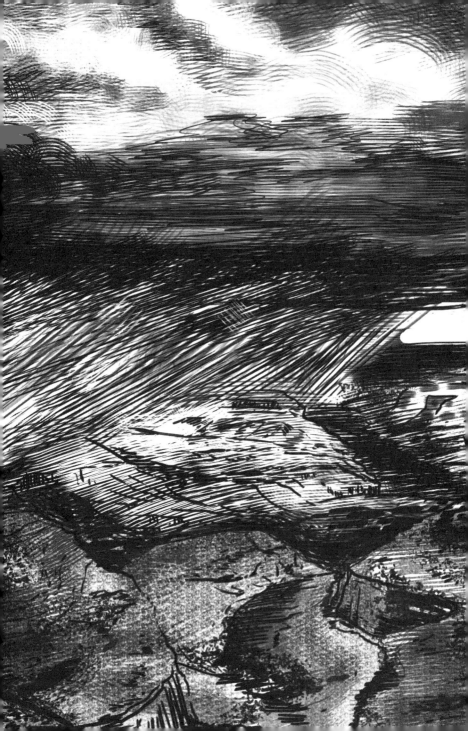

Winter rains also collect in cracks in the canyon walls and freeze. Water expands when it freezes, making the cracks wider. Finally, the rock breaks off from the canyon wall and crashes to the bottom.

Rainwater erosion also washes away softer layers of rock that have supported harder rock. The harder rock loosens and eventually falls down into the canyon.

Wind has also played a part in shaping the canyon. Many of the mesas and buttes that are so amazing to see were formed by millions of years of wind brushing tiny bits of rock away one bit at a time.

Mesas and Buttes

A mesa is a flat-topped hill or mountain with very steep sides. It is always wider than it is tall. The word "mesa" means "table" in Spanish.

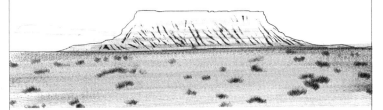

Buttes are smaller than mesas. They are taller than they are wide. Both mesas and buttes are found throughout the southwestern United States.

Because of all the erosion, visitors to the Grand Canyon today can see at least eleven different layers of rock. These layers lie one right on top of another, like a layer cake. The oldest rocks are the bottom layer, and the youngest, the top.

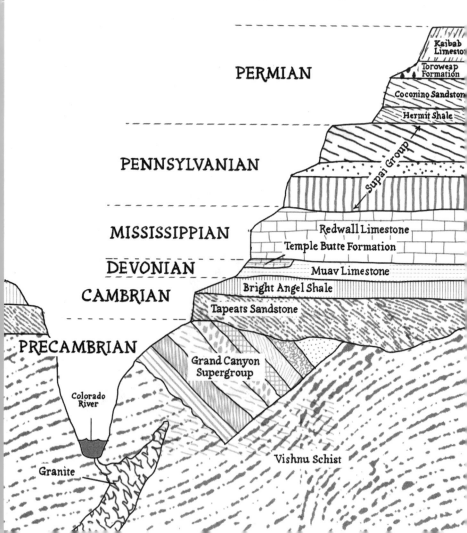

PERMIAN

Kaibab Limeston

Toroweap Formation

Coconino Sandston

Hermit Shale

PENNSYLVANIAN

Supai Group

MISSISSIPPIAN

Redwall Limestone

Temple Butte Formation

DEVONIAN

Muav Limestone

CAMBRIAN

Bright Angel Shale

Tapeats Sandstone

PRECAMBRIAN

Grand Canyon Supergroup

Colorado River

Vishnu Schist

Granite

The oldest rock is called the Vishnu Schist. It is 1.7 billion years old and mostly black in color. The next oldest layer consists of pink sedimentary and igneous rock. It is between 800 million and 1.2 billion years old.

On top of the pink rock is a layer called the Tapeats Sandstone. It is packed with fossilized sponges and other sea creatures. These are proof that an ocean covered the area 545 million years ago.

On top of that layer is shale. It's blue gray in color and is 515 million years old. The shale is topped by limestone containing tiny bits of shells. Again this is evidence of another prehistoric ocean. The next layer, the Temple Butte Formation, which is a purplish limestone, also has many marine fossils.

At this point the canyon walls become much steeper. The next layer, which consists of more limestone, is eight hundred feet high and was formed 340 million years ago. Although it is mainly silver gray, iron oxide in the rocks has stained parts a deep red.

Topping this thick layer is a mix of sandstone, shale, and siltstone. In it are fossils of insects and ferns. Just above that is more shale, and then sandstone from dunes 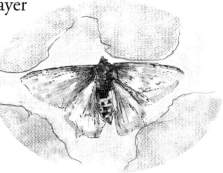 of a desert that covered the plateau 275 million years ago. It, in turn, is covered by the darker yellow-gray Toroweap Formation made of gypsum and shale and some sandstone. The very top layer of the plateau is cream-colored limestone.

In his journal, John Wesley Powell often wrote about the amazing rock formations and layers of rock that he and his group passed by. Most of his observations were precise and written in scientific language. But occasionally his writing becomes poetic. When he came upon beds of lava he wrote, "What a conflict of water and fire there must have been here! Just imagine a river of molten rock, running down into a river of melted snow. What a seething and boiling of the waters; what clouds of steam rolled into the heavens."

What's in a Name?

The Grand Canyon has thousands of rock masterpieces, and many of the most famous ones have names. Some are named after explorers, like Powell Point and Cardenas Butte.

Many are named after Native American tribes—Hopi Point, Pima Point, Yavapai Point, Coconino Plateau, Comanche Point, and Navajo Point.

There are also names from ancient Egypt, like Osiris Temple and Isis Temple. And a whole group take their names from the legends of King Arthur and the Knights of the Round Table—Lancelot Point, Guinevere Castle, Gawain Abyss, Galahad Point, King Arthur Castle, and Holy Grail Temple.

ISIS TEMPLE

CHAPTER 6
Wildlife in the Canyon

First-time visitors usually are blown away by the sight of the canyon itself. All the rock! They are unaware of the incredible number of animals and plants that make the Grand Canyon their home.

Riding the canyon's swirling air currents are bald eagles, ravens, red-tailed hawks, turkey vultures, and other birds of prey, which are also called "raptors." Every year in September and October, National Park Service rangers lead groups of bird-watchers to identify and count various types of raptors flying over the canyon.

In addition to the raptors, there are 350 different species of birds that fly over or live inside the canyon.

At the bottom of the canyon, there are seventeen kinds of freshwater fish that live in the Colorado River or its feeder streams. There are forty-seven reptile species, including geckos, lizards, Gila monsters, iguanas, and three kinds of rattlesnakes.

Mountain lion

Gila monster

There are all kinds of mammals, from small creatures such as chipmunks, squirrels, mice, weasels, porcupines, raccoons, and bats to big bears, elk, deer, sheep, mountain lions, and mule deer.

Depending on the time of year, visitors might glimpse elk near Grand Canyon Village. They are called Roosevelt elk and were brought to Grand Canyon Park after a native species of elk was killed off by hunters in the early 1900s.

Roosevelt elk

For thousands of years, people have hunted bighorn sheep, mountain lions, black bears, and mule deer in and around the Grand Canyon. The mountain lions also hunt the elk and deer. In fact, naturalists say that the average mountain lion kills one deer or elk per week at the canyon. This keeps the elk and deer population under control so they will have enough food to eat.

At night thousands of bats emerge from caves in the canyon's walls and consume tons of flying insects.

Only in the Canyon

The pink Grand Canyon rattlesnake is found nowhere else in the world. The snake can grow to over four feet long and has a unique pink color. That allows it to blend in with rocks of the same color in the lower canyon.

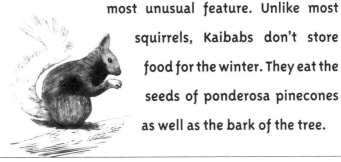

Besides the pink rattlesnake, there is also a species of squirrel—the Kaibab squirrel—that is found only in the canyon and only on its North Rim. Kaibabs are light gray in color with black bellies and snow-white tails. Long tasseled ears are its most unusual feature. Unlike most squirrels, Kaibabs don't store food for the winter. They eat the seeds of ponderosa pinecones as well as the bark of the tree.

The most dangerous animal in the Grand Canyon—at least, to tourists—is a small, furry, cute creature called the rock squirrel. Rock squirrels gather in busy areas because they use humans as vending machines.

Tourists try to lure the squirrels for pictures by holding out nuts, sandwiches, fruit, and other treats. Often tourists end up getting bitten. Besides being painful, squirrel bites can transmit disease and cause bad infections.

Although people don't usually use the color green to describe the Grand Canyon, it is home to 1,750 plant species. That is more than in any other

Grizzly-bear prickly pear

national park in the United States. Cliff-rose, Apache plume, grizzly-bear prickly pear, mariposa lily, and desert columbine bloom throughout the canyon and give it color.

One reason for the variety of plants and trees is the many different climates within the canyon. The canyon is so deep that the climate changes depending on where visitors are.

Each different climate supports different kinds of plants and animals. This is what is known as a biotic community—a group of plants and animals that live together in a certain area. There are six different biotic communities within the canyon.

They too are stacked one on top of another like layers in a gigantic cake.

At the floor of the inner canyon, the climate is desert-like. In the summer the temperature may reach over 105 degrees. The floor gets only eight inches of rain a year, so desert plants like cacti and yucca thrive there.

Agave plants bloom once every fifteen to twenty-five years. They are found deep in the canyon. The plant's flowers, leaves, stalks, and sap can all be eaten. It is sometimes called the "century plant" because it takes so long to bloom. The banana yucca blooms every two or three years and produces a fruit that tastes a bit like bananas.

The creatures that live on the canyon floor, such as kangaroo rats, desert iguanas, and cactus mice, have also adapted to the harsh environment. They can survive in extremely hot, dry weather.

A very different biotic community is found on the canyon's North Rim. It is covered with pine

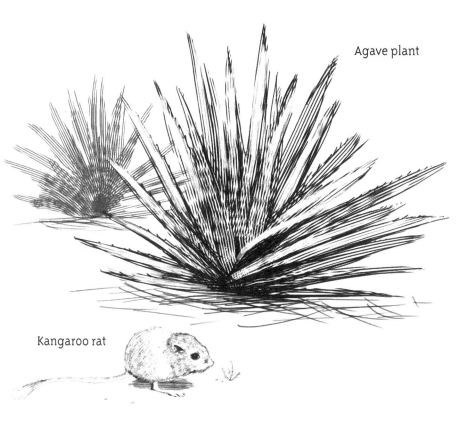

Agave plant

Kangaroo rat

trees and is home to mountain lions, elk, and bighorn sheep. The North Rim gets an average of thirty inches of rain and snow every year. That's a lot. In fact there is so much snow on the North Rim of the Grand Canyon that it is closed to tourists from October to May. All that precipitation, however, is necessary for ponderosa pines, Douglas firs, and spruce. The roots take hold in cracks in the sandstone so that the trees can grow.

Many North Rim animals could not survive in the hot desert conditions of the canyon floor. Likewise, the plants and animals that thrive deep down in the canyon would not survive the rainy, cold North Rim winters. Although the difference in climate is like traveling from Mexico to Canada, amazingly these biotic communities are only a mile apart!

CHAPTER 7
A Trip to the Grand Canyon

Visiting the Grand Canyon is amazing—and frustrating. It's amazing because there are so many sights and so many interesting things to do. (If you've never ridden a mule, you can do that at the Grand Canyon.) But it's frustrating to go there because the Grand Canyon is so huge that seeing only a little bit of it can take two or three days. People visit the Grand Canyon year after year and never see all of it.

You are
here

Most visitors, especially the first time, go to the South Rim. It is much easier to get to than the isolated North Rim. It also offers a greater choice of things to do and see. Inside the visitor center there is an information desk staffed by park rangers who can answer questions about the park.

The first thing, of course, is to stop and take a good long look. The Grand Canyon Visitor Center on the South Rim by Mather Point is a popular stopping point. The view from there encompasses almost a third of the Grand Canyon.

Before You Go

If you and your family are planning to visit the Grand Canyon, spend some time planning your trip in advance. Visit the National Park Service Grand Canyon website at www.nps.gov/grca. It gives lots of suggestions about how to get to the Grand Canyon, where to stay, and what sights are of special interest. The website also has photos, slide shows, maps, and multimedia presentations.

Mather Point also overlooks one of the widest parts of the canyon. (Remember, if you're visiting during the busy summer months, you may encounter big crowds all along the South Rim. There is plenty of parking away from the rim.)

There are free shuttle buses on the South Rim. The buses take four different routes. Using the shuttle buses is a good way to visit the most-popular spots. It is especially helpful during the busy summer season when one of the roads is closed to regular traffic.

Grand Canyon Village has hosted visitors for over one hundred years. When the Santa Fe Railroad first reached the South Rim in 1901, people finally had an easy way to travel to the Grand Canyon. That's when tourism really began.

At the top of the Bright Angel Trail, visitors cannot miss seeing a rambling frame house with a sign that says *Kolb Studio*. The Kolb brothers, Ellsworth and Emery, also deserve some of the credit for turning the Grand Canyon into a popular vacation spot. In 1902, they started photographing tourists starting their mule trips into the canyon.

Once each group left, one of the brothers, usually Emery, would take the exposed film and scramble nearly five miles down the Bright Angel Trail to where there was freshwater that they needed for processing the film. After developing and printing the pictures in a darkroom they had built there, Emery would walk back up the very steep trail and sell the pictures to the returning tourists.

The Kolbs also roamed throughout the canyon photographing the natural wonders that most tourists could not get to. They sold those pictures in their studio.

In the winter of 1911–1912, Ellsworth and Emery retraced John Wesley Powell's journey down the Colorado through the canyon. They made movies of their trip. In later years they toured the United States, showing the film and encouraging everyone to come and see the Grand Canyon. And many did!

Today the Kolb Studio is a gift shop, bookstore, and art gallery.

In the 1920s and '30s, the architect Mary Jane Colter designed six beautiful buildings for the park. Back then it was unusual for a woman to be an architect. Mary Jane Colter was a very talented one. She took great pains to design buildings that reflected the Native American history of the Southwest. In fact, she became an expert on Native American customs, art, and jewelry.

Colter designed Hermit's Rest, Desert View Watchtower, and the Lookout Studio to give visitors great places from which to view the Grand Canyon. Lookout Studio is in Grand

Lookout Studio

Canyon Village. Hermit's Rest is seven miles west of the village. Both blend into the canyon landscape so perfectly that it is easy to miss them at first. The rocks in the stone walls are laid horizontally and echo the rim's rock layers. The Desert View Watchtower is twenty-five miles east of the canyon. It looks like an authentic Native American structure, as does Hopi House, the gift shop designed by Colter that is right in the village.

Colter designed two famous hotels at the Grand Canyon—Bright Angel Lodge and Phantom Ranch. Bright Angel Lodge is right in the village. However, Phantom Ranch is at the bottom of the canyon at the base of the Bright Angel Trail. While Phantom Ranch was being built, Colter had to take a five-and-a-half-hour mule ride down to get to the construction site. All the materials for the ranch, except for stones, had to be carried down by mules.

Mary Jane Colter

Besides the six notable buildings in Grand Canyon National Park, Colter designed hotels, restaurants, and shops throughout the southwest United States.

She was born in 1869 in Pittsburgh, Pennsylvania, and studied at the California School of Design in San Francisco. In 1902 she took a summer job with the Fred Harvey Company, which was working with the Santa Fe Railroad building hotels and restaurants. In 1910 she began working for the Harvey Company full-time. Mary Jane Colter designed many other buildings outside the Grand Canyon, but sadly only a few remain. La Posada Hotel in nearby Winslow, Arizona, is the finest of them. She died in 1958.

Mule rides remain a popular way to see the Grand Canyon. Mules have carried supplies and people to the bottom of the canyon and back for over a century. Besides overnight trips to Phantom Ranch, there are shorter mule rides along the rim trail.

Hiking and camping are both popular pastimes in the Grand Canyon. They offer a great way to take in the natural beauty of the area "below the rim."

The most popular hiking route is the Bright Angel Trail. It starts in Grand Canyon Village and twists and turns for 9.9 miles until it reaches Bright Angel Creek and the Colorado River.

The route is steep and the trail has no guardrails. Hikers must wear good shoes or boots and carry plenty of water because of the extremely high temperatures at the canyon floor.

Even longtime hikers do not try to go down to the river and back in one day. It is also possible to take shorter hikes on the Bright Angel Trail with turnarounds at 1.5-, 3-, and 5-mile points.

Other popular hiking routes are the South Kaibab Trail, Hermit Trail, and Grandview Trail. The easiest trail is the Rim Trail; it goes from Grand Canyon Village to Hermit's Rest. It is flat and even paved in some places. Hikers can catch the shuttle bus back to the village if they get tired.

There are two main campsites on the South Rim, one at Mather Point and the other at Desert View. These sites are operated by the National Park Service and fill up during the busy summer months. Spots at Mather Point can be reserved

through the National Park Service.

Another popular camping site is at Havasu Falls on the Havasupai Indian Reservation. After hiking ten miles down into the canyon, campers pitch their tents next to Havasu Creek.

The North Rim of the Grand Canyon is much more isolated than the South Rim. It has only one hotel, the Grand Canyon Lodge, and one campground. The North Rim is also at a higher altitude than the South Rim and gets much more rain and snow. The North Rim is only open from May 15 to October 15.

Every year thousands of adventurous tourists take raft trips through part or all of the Grand Canyon. The Colorado is a much tamer river now than when John Wesley Powell led his group through the canyon. That's because the Glen Canyon Dam regulates the amount of water in the river.

Seeing the Grand Canyon from a raft is very different from seeing it from the North or South Rims. The canyon walls really seem towering; they look much taller when you gaze up at them from the canyon bottom rather than looking down at them from the rim. And although there are many white-water rapids along the route, experienced guides make rafting trips safe and fun.

CHAPTER 8
The Hand of Man

It is easy to visit the Grand Canyon and think that except for a few buildings here and there, humans have left it alone. But that is not true. The Colorado River has been tamed by dams built at each end of the Grand Canyon. Hoover Dam on the Arizona-Nevada border created a gigantic reservoir called Lake Mead. Lake Mead has flooded the western end of the canyon. It is 112 miles long and over 500 feet deep. The fierce Separation Rapids that so frightened John Wesley Powell and his men were buried by Lake Mead.

At the eastern end of the Grand Canyon is Glen Canyon Dam. It was completed in 1963, and has had a major impact on the canyon's ecology. Many of the canyon's natural sand beaches have disappeared. Spring flooding used

to bring new sand down to the beaches. Now that sand is caught behind the dam.

Water is released into the canyon every day. The amount varies depending on how much electricity is needed by the dam's customers. The water has an average temperature of forty-five degrees winter and summer. That's cold!

The humpback chub, a native fish, was able to survive the cold water in winter, but it needed warmer water in the summer for spawning (mating). The fish had to find smaller, warmer side streams to spawn. As a result there are only a few thousand humpback chub, a fish that has lived in the Grand Canyon for three to five million years.

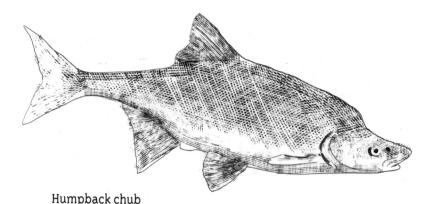

Humpback chub

Now the Park Service is taking steps to protect the humpback chub. It is moving some chub to other streams where the fish will have a better chance at spawning.

Three other species of fish native to the Grand Canyon were not so lucky. The Colorado pikeminnow, roundtail chub, and bonytail have disappeared from the area entirely.

The Grand Canyon's popularity has also created problems. Over a million cars and buses bring tourists to the Grand Canyon each year. In the busy summer months all those vehicles create traffic jams and pollute the air. There are many more people who would like to camp than there are campsites, and keeping the campsites clean and litter-free is not always easy.

In recent years, the Park Service has created a master plan to manage all the visitors. People must park away from the canyon and take shuttle buses to the popular sites on the South Rim. Hikers are no longer able to buy water in disposable plastic bottles anywhere in the park. Camping permits must be obtained in advance, and there is a long waiting list for permits to take private trips down the Colorado. This is to make sure that there are never too many people in the canyon.

President Theodore Roosevelt understood that it is a crime (he called it "vandalism") "to destroy or to permit the destruction of what is beautiful in nature, whether it be a cliff, a forest, or a species of mammal or bird." The rules set down by the Park Service will help keep the Grand Canyon beautiful for everyone now and in the future.

Timeline of the Grand Canyon

bya= billion years ago, mya=million years ago

1.7 bya	Vishnu Schist forms
1.2 bya–740 mya	Grand Canyon Supergroup forms
515 mya	Bright Angel Shale forms
340 mya	Redwall Limestone forms
280 mya	Hermit Shale forms
270 mya	Kaibab Limestone forms
60 mya	Colorado Plateau begins to form
6 mya	Colorado River begins eroding the Colorado Plateau to form the Grand Canyon
10,000 years ago	First humans visit the Grand Canyon (Paleo-Indians)
500	Anasazi begin visiting the Grand Canyon
1540	First Europeans (Spanish) reach the Grand Canyon
1869	John Wesley Powell explores the Grand Canyon
1884	John Hance becomes the first white man to settle at the Grand Canyon
1901–1909	Theodore Roosevelt is president of the United States; he later becomes known as the "conservation president"
1901	Santa Fe Railroad reaches the Grand Canyon
1905	El Tovar Hotel opens
	Mary June Colter begins designing buildings in the area that will become Grand Canyon National Park
1908	Roosevelt creates Grand Canyon National Monument
1919	Grand Canyon named national park
1936	Hoover Dam completed; Lake Mead begins to form
1963	Glen Canyon Dam completed; Colorado River is "tamed"

Timeline of the World

bya= billion years ago, mya=million years ago

Sponges and jellyfish drift in the sea –
Worms, the first creatures with –
nervous systems, begin to appear
The entire land surface of the earth merges into –
a single continent, known as Pangea
"Continental drift" results in our present –
arrangement of six continents
Mammals appear on earth –
Dinosaurs die out for still-unconfirmed reasons –
Australia becomes a separate land mass –
Various ape species develop the ability to walk upright –
A species of human in east Africa, *Homo erectus*, is –
probably the first identifiable ancestor of modern man
Humans first walk to the Americas across a land bridge –
joining Asia and North America
Hernando Cortés defeats the Aztecs at Tenochtitlan –
Abraham Lincoln takes office as the sixteenth –
president of the United States
World War I begins –
Construction on the Golden Gate Bridge begins –
The state of Israel is officially created –
The first airplane lands at the geographic North Pole –
Fidel Castro leads a revolution in Cuba –
Nelson Mandela is jailed in white-ruled South Africa –

Bibliography

Berke, Arnold. *Mary Colter, Architect of the Southwest.* New York: Princeton Architectural Press, 2002.

Dolnick, Edward. *Down the Great Unknown: John Wesley Powell's 1869 Journey of Discovery and Tragedy Through the Grand Canyon*. New York: HarperCollins, 2001.

Fishbein, Seymour L. *Grand Canyon Country: Its Majesty and Its Lore*. Washington, DC: National Geographic Society, 2011.

Kaiser, James. *Grand Canyon: The Complete Guide: Grand Canyon National Park*. Chicago: Destination Press, 2011.

Newman, Lance, ed. *The Grand Canyon Reader*. Berkeley: University of California Press, 2002.

Website

United States National Park Service, Grand Canyon National Park www.nps.gov/grca/